WITHDRAWN

if I could
sleep deeply
enough

BY VASSAR MILLER

if I could sleep deeply enough

poems
by Vassar Miller

LIVERIGHT   *New York*

The author gratefully acknowledges the editors
of the following journals in which certain
poems in this book first appeared: *Antioch Review,
Hiram Poetry Review, Latitudes, New York Quarterly,
Pulse, Stone Drum, Toward Winter, Unicorn Folios,*
and *Whetstone.*

Liveright, 386 Park Avenue South
New York, New York 10016

1.987654321
Library of Congress Cataloging in Publication Data

Miller, Vassar.
If I could sleep deeply enough.

I. Title.
PS3525.I56351I4   811'.5'4   74-13320
ISBN 0-87140-607-1
ISBN 0-87140-099-5 (pbk.)

Manufactured in the United States of America

For Robert Bonazzi
in gratitude and friendship

CONTENTS

vii

Introduction to a Poetry Reading

I was born with my mod dress sewn onto my body,
stitched to my flesh,
basted into my bones.
I could never, somehow, take it all off
to wash the radical dirt out.
I even carry my own rock
hard in my mouth,
grinding it out bit by bit.
So, bear me
as I bear you,
high, in the grace of greeting.

1

Cycle

My body, weary traveler,
in an oasis drinks
from pools of sleep.

Its cells, all its million tongues,
lap up the dark coolness.
Never love went

more naked to bed than when
my body shrugs off
logic's gold sheath

in the black irrational,
water which one day
will drink my body.

After a Blackness

Just come up from near drowning—
I brush the water from my eyes,
blow my nose.

Better from an aesthetic
viewpoint to have finished the job.
Yet who lives by

such a windy diet? If
my mirror gives me as good as
it gets, fine!

But you do see me? You're certain?

Another Day

The day, damp bird, mopes on its branch where leaves
still cling with wizened fists above
the lawns all blanched the color of stale vomit.

The day drops dead, time's tune inside my skull
droning toward sleep when I lie down
lonely to lust's one-finger exercise.

Diary

Day gambols up to my bed like a dog
with the sunshine clenched between its teeth
and wagging a windy tail.
"Go away," I grumble and push it aside
and burrow my head under the covers
from the rump of the waking minutes.
But it is too late. The slippery quarry of sleep has vanished
down the rivers of darkness—
prey that has held me captive like some mythical wolf-child
suckled by tits of a four-footed mother.
Now being doubly orphaned, I roam here and there
searching the aisles of a half-dream, through the thickets of
      idleness,
in a lapsing of thought down a byway of silence
until light settles and fades
like froth on a glass of beer
in whose brown peace I brood, becoming
a shadow watching the shadows.

Nervous Night

Rain walks down the wind
in soft shoes,
and chortles in the deep holes of the earth.

Earth pads through my heart
on socked paws,
and chuckles from the red cave of my blood.

Blood strums through my veins,
that brisk hive,
and jabbers out the hiss and hum of atoms.

Insomniac's Prayer

I lie with my body knotted into a fist
clenching against itself,
arms doubled against my ribs
knees crooking into a gnarl,
legs, side by side, martialed.

My sleep is a war against waking up,
my waking up is a slow raveling again into dark
when dreams jump out of my skull
like pictures in a child's pop-up book
onto paper if my luck can catch them
before they dribble away into dingy dawns.

Oh, who will unsnarl my body
into gestures of love?
Who will give my heart room
to fly free in its rickety cage?
Whose subtlety whisper apart my legs,
thrusting quick like a snake's tongue?
Who will nudge the dreams back into my head,
back into my bones, where rhyming with one another
like wind chimes,
they will make music whenever I move?

Brief Victory

At your soft word my night
shimmers a moment
in a rise of light,

and for a breath's suspense
I walk the waters
of your innocence.

My will one heartbeat lingers
a wash of sand
winnowed by your fingers.

Lying in Bed Late

As though I held a lover hard inside me
I keep the darkness locked behind my lashes
To seed my flesh with sleep, my head with dreams,
Pulsing to melody within my blood,
Making my stiff bones burgeon like green branches.
But now the tides are ebbing out of me,
Withdrawing from the coastlines of my lashes
Whose telltale dampness hints my heart elsewhere
When I go through the empty morning bruising
My shins upon the edges of the light.
Somnambulist with staring eyes, my mind
Broods on the soft black washes of those waters
Swept through me nightly and by day receding
Still echoed in the seashell of my body.

Tired

If I could
sleep deeply enough,
I might touch the eye
of dark, life.

Yet the way
I sleep, men drink salt.
Always wearier
upon waking—

I have written
these lines without book,
thumbing the thesaurus
of my bones.

2

Refugees

We walk through a lean land
where love goes hungry to protest
its grubby works.

We walk through a cold country,
where love strips naked, shucking off
its own sweet lies.

We walk through a shrewd snare
where love starves, gambling with its guts
as poker chips.

We walk through a harsh highland
where love drinks dwindling air and panics.
This rush of rock—!

Age of Aquarius, Age of Assassins

For George Wallace

Conniver, my nonkissing cousin, bastard, my brother,
this poet bereft of heroes and slightly below
the angels, and therefore Satan's small sister salutes you
to question, Which land shall I leave now and head for
    what other?
From people committing such crimes where should I go
without sloughing the human skin in whose guise a crank
    shoots you?

When A-bombs, H-bombs, the whole alphabet of our guilt
indicts me no more than the ovens roasting the Jews,
no more than my cronies' mutual murder by inches?
You, more petty than yesterday's paper, what have we built
since one week, two weeks ago, since Adam was news,
but the House of the Shoe Fitting Best the Harder it
    Pinches!

Not that I with precision tools could construct the house
    better
than you, driving wooden pegs with your stone-headed
    hatchet.
For man is a chronic case regressing, improving,
regressing, twisting in bed to find a cool spot, turned bitter
when he finds the sheet burning again where his bones
    touch it.
Yet, there's some hope (though, by God, none to you)
    because he keeps moving.

Culture Shock

We have gone to the moon.
We have burned the hair of a goat.
We have offered the heart of a chicken
to the two-faced demon
who scratches himself in the darkness.
We have gone to the moon.

We have gone to the moon.
We have spoken to angels
of unspeakable matters
that would burn up your ears if you understood them.
And our lips are afoam with the holy spittle.
We have gone to the moon.

We have gone to the moon.
We have sat holding hands in a circle
so touching the shapes without hands
when great Uncle Hubert says he is lonesome but happy
with things that go bump in the night.
We have gone to the moon.

We have gone to the moon.
We do not go out in the days when the stars are against us.
We plan parties and journeys when the stars are right,
say Yes or say No as they direct us.
Our souls are strung up by wires to the zodiac.
We have gone to the moon.

December Afternoon

The leaves, midway in their turning,
hàve slumped from green into brown,
bleached of an elegant death.

Over their brittle corpses
creeps the damp flag of air,
the wind chime hanging, tear on the crone's cheek

of winter whose branches with bony fingers
clutching its scrawny body
cradles Christ close, unlikely secret.

First Snow in Ten Years

I fall awake into a vacuum
leashed from my drowsing
by a bird's startled squawk.

My thoughts nose the air like a sleepy hound.
No need to look
because my mind is snowing.

Winter Song Without Music

The sky leaks rain
onto the washed-out grass.
Birds sulk on the branches
like inverted raindrops.
They will not die, not freeze
to anything
except a wet gray shiver.

Hurricane Watch

The trees have deserted us,
dogs hunkered down,
motionless, ears laid back.

The air has deserted us,
slumped like a corpse
to the pit of the lungs.

The insects have deserted us,
winged whispers muted
into timbres of terror.

Nature has deserted us,
a woman sloughing
off her body by frenzy.

Silence has deserted us,
absence of noise
less than heart's annihilation.

Faux Pas

I sat with you in a back pew when
your father died; for you, stared at so long,
would not gape at the helpless dead.

At your mother's funeral I thought to sit
in the same place beside you, decent as always
to the point of fault. Who would have guessed!

Dear friend, forgive my unaverted eyes.
But there's no back row of the mind to hide
here from the horror of your dying.

A Mourning for Miss Rose

The questions in her mind
were all brained birds
which she could not remember,
calling and screeching.

Their corpses littered her thoughts
and choked her dreams,
entangled the roots of her tongue,
stuffed her with silence.

So, when she died we scattered
the old easy answers over her coffin,
but the birds revived and flew out of her mouth
screaming their scorn.

Letter to Friends Dead and Living

I

You always liked death,
and no one could do
a damn thing about it.

You walked in hand
across the street with it,
lover and friend and angel

you called it. Well good,
We're seldom so lucky
as to get what we want.

II

Stay as sweet as you are
hanging loose while you strangle
in a dangle of nerve.

because old Ben Franklin,
that cool cat who said gray cats
look alike in the dark,

proclaimed, "If we do not
hang together, we shall
hang separately," so

said Pastor Bonhoeffer,
dividing the Word of Truth
raveled out to rope's end.

III

I write in a rage,
sitting in silence,
music burning my bones

Lord God, keep my cool,
for I cannot
without freezing to death—

such singers at dark
walk down my hall,
whisper, "Wake up and feel

Lament

No girl will he clothe golden in her womanhood,
moving inside her, lithe young animal.
Lament with me that he is only for the mirror
shattered into the teeth that tear his pride,
the flag of the defeated caught on brambles.

He, wholly run to flesh, becomes abstraction
to copulate with dreams and bed with shadows.
Lament with me that he buys nothing, owning
only a single sided coin, burning his pocket empty
until he dances to the sound of one hand clapping.

She who would wait for him will long lie lonely.
He passes her room to pump abandoned wells.
Lament with me that he fishes from dry gulches,
his brave rod useless, and if she hears a knocking
upon her door it is the wind's cold knuckles.

Good Counsel, Rarely Heeded

Lie still—the shy beasts
will lap the pool
of your attention,

its water be signed
with the quick scrawls
of their swift shadows.

3

A Wistfulness

I wish I had loved you
without knowing,
had touched your face, curious
what it was blossomed under my fingers,

like Adam—bright shapes, lions,
fawns, colts, bears,
nameless, playing around him,
Oh, long before he knew he was naked.

Thanksgiving After Holy Communion

You come to me like a bird
lighting upon my palm,
nesting upon my tongue,
flying through the branches of my being
into the forest of my darkness.

Your wings have troubled my atoms,
set intangibles striking
together in crystal music
as the light flowers out of my body
as my body bloomed from the light.

Love Song for Easter Even

Just for a moment now I feel immortal.
I lie on the grass with you. Its green awash
like seaweed under water. The long flash
of sky above us, blue jay's wing. Lush chortle
of birdsong in the leaves. No noise to startle,
but only soothe me here. I have no wish
to lie here still, with the sun's flush
light on my skin this way, forever gentle.

Just for a moment—hush, love!—I have quit
the binds and bonds of the body inside matter.
My bones are supple as a baby's—look!—my flesh
finds not a single flaw, seems infinite,
like Christ, can tread the tips of the grass like water.
Yet you dart past my touch like Him, smooth fish!

High Noon

Summer unwinds itself like time's green tape
slowed down a little till the eye
may catch what other time flies by,
so we may feel its texture and its shape;
may store up the sweet sizzle in the trees,
the cicadas' antiphonal choirs
one memory's and one desire's;
hold clouds piled high in a cumulous frieze
depicting dreams against the arched blue air,
when earth falls silent in the spell
of noon's suspended syllable,
and it is finer than a feast to stare
caught in the yellow honey of the heat.
Handle most gently what one day
the heart will ache in vain to stay—
such minutes swifter than its ebbing beat.

Church in Heidelberg

You have been sleeping well six hundred years,
master and mistress, peacefully
smiling here, carved in effigy.
Even your dog smiles, snuggling at your feet,
as if he found it sweet
to have his wan, wild breath
domesticated into death.
Had you no children? Was that cause for tears?
Or were you much content to age alone
when lust had simmered down, yet stayed as good
essential as your daily food
digested into dark, to be considered like this stone
I touch now without embarrassment or riot
or envy of you for any gift save quiet.
And still you slept on while the Crusades roared
While many Masses hummed about your bed
with many *Misereres* for the dead
whose pity men had better sought instead.
Then when stern Luther howled about his Lord
of terrible mercy, still you never stirred,
but smiled away as though you kept
a joke between you while you slept.

Posthumous Letter to Thomas Merton

Unlike you who discovered solitude
To be "Forerunner of the Word of God,"
I search and find it no more than the soul's
Chafing against itself like any dog
Rubbing its mangy rump against a tree.
I might have asked you how to bridge the gap
Between our two alonenesses, between
Yours, self-elected, freely chosen, and
Mine blindly blundered into from the womb,
At first not even seen for what it was,
And then, once recognized, raged at, kicked at,
And cursed. Perhaps there is a gulf between them,
The gulf dividing mind to which God is
A harmony, from mind to which God seems
The discord, shattering tidy tunes of thought,
Yet no, devout monk though you were, your God
Was not a mystery emasculated,
Poked at through barbed wire meshes of the creeds,
Led out well-groomed and curried for the faithful
To adulate from their safe vantage point.
Now that your words have smoked away to silence,
I dare not put an answer on your tongue,
As though a devotee had stuffed your mouth
With speeches that you never made. I only
Write you these lines, less poem than presumption,
Addressed in care of my bewilderment.
I ask you, self-styled marginal man,
Do not we sufferers always inhabit
The edges of the world as pioneers
To prove how much humanity can bear
And still be human, experimenters in
The bloody laboratory of our lives.
Taking and testing every pain tossed from
The pulsing cosmos, fragments we reshape,
As best as the materials allow,
To buttress God's cathedrals built from chaos?

A Sadness

I see so many drawn and tense,
taut against pain, arched in anger, flexed
with fury, faces wizened into fists.
And yet so many have been washed with love
from head to foot,
their bodies should shine golden with it.

It flows like sunshine down the skin,
like a soft spill of yellow grain,
like the dust from a crumble of rose petals,
a fabric finer than webs of wind spun
over the world.
Yet none may wear it for a garment.

4

Valse Triste

I am serious, sisters,
weaving my songs
with the black widow spiders'.

I am deadly, my brothers,
serious—death,
that primeval black humor.

I am joking, good mothers,
aping your clowns
with black cracks in their grins.

I am clowning, dumb fathers,
dandled in dust's
black seamy tuxedo.

Dry Season

My thoughts, mute birds on thorny boughs of silence
Sulking with drooping wings,
Moulting their feathers, maintain a breathless balance,
And not one sings.

With their bright music all the air once shimmered.
Now they are snared in hush.
The leaves where they in a green sunlight summered
Are a dead brush.

The air is sickroom still. Like a black nit
Each moment makes its climb
Up a steep pause of wind. For bitter grit
The birds eat time.

On the Examination Table

My eyes, two birds
crazily threshing
in the trap of their sockets,

my tongue, dry leaf
ready to fall
to the pit of my throat,

my breath, fragile moth
caught in a cave-in
of my gullet's tight tunnel,

my belly, overturned turtle,
stripped from the shell
of daily decorum,

my body, dull dog,
shies into terror's
mythical monster.

Spastics

(First poem from Handi-Lib)

They are not beautiful, young, and strong when it strikes,
but wizened in wombs like everyone else,
like monkeys,
like fish,
like worms,
creepy-crawlies from yesterday's rocks
tomorrow will step on.

Hence presidents, and most parents, don't have to worry
No one in congress will die of it. No one else.
Don't worry.
They just
hang on
drooling, stupid from watching too much TV,
born-that-way senile,

rarely marry, expected to make it with Jesus,
never really make it at all,
don't know how,
some can't
feed themselves,
fool with, *well*— Even some sappy saint said they
look young because pure.

Confession at a Friends' Meeting

Thoughts paddle in the floods of silence,
no single spar of sound to cling to,
except the rumble of my neighbor's belly,
the creaking of his shoes,

only my tears to serve as notes
upon the staff of unflawed air
for all the selves born, battered by
waters bearing none home.

Heart flails among those billows, washed
half away, uncentering down
in love saying itself without
a word, singing past music.

Enlightened Selfishness

(A second confession at a Friends' Meeting)

A nail is driving me down
into my own silence.
This can't be how it's done.

Chairs scrape. Guts growl. Here, of course,
Nobody sings bad hymns.
But what if someone . . .? Oh, well,

some meadowlark, outside, carols
making do for Bach,
who was, by the way, extremely

prolific with children and music,
theology
so much better than mandrakes.

My silence tingles, murks up
its pristine waters,
all of which only proves

it's scary, to say the least,
riding hobby horses
to death—friendly gray ones even.

Now You See Me, Now . . .

How I race
on the back of a beast
rearing high on a heatwave's footless hold!

I must fall,
I must sink, must go down,
smothered inside his red belly of rage.

The Irresistible Urge

What flies up in my face like a bird out of the grass,
clearing the coop of my caption,
why like a deer in a thicket hiding,
like a tiger among the branches crouching
where is enough to hold it here
firm in my fingers,
on the tip of my taste,
in an angle of eyesight,
an inch from my ear.
Summoned, my five senses pay court
too courteous for a question

(till the thicket trembles,
till the branches snap!).

Sow's Ear

I turn my life over and over
like a toy windmill or a doll.
From whatever angle I view it,
I find my death.

I measure it, weigh it, and try it.
Yet its molecules and atoms
will not add up to anything
except my death.

I may fling it over my shoulder
like a sweater almost forgotten.
Still I feel it tugged by each breeze
cold from my death.

Nobody would care except me.
Why even I should, who can say—
delicate monster, its edges
frayed toward my death!

Fantasia

Last night I lay writing a poem,
lifting barely a finger.
I did not need to.

You did it for me, my dear,
typing on me with your
invisible teeth.

I've counted your phrases, one
on my forehead and cheeks,
two on my mouth,

three on my breasts and my belly,
printing my mons veneris,
touching those places,

shadows, privates, genitals,
gentlest now if my fists
open with poems.

You with your long dusty hair
draping my shoulders, hiding
what does not need

any longer to be hidden.
Read my face and my hands
stripped raw like Jesus.

Wraith of my dead mother coming
down the hallways of midnight
with the dishcloth

she slapped my father with once,
Veronica of the Kitchen.
Never be shocked—

Only the book-ghosts can scare us,
not the real ones, their footsteps
crooked and lurching.

Impasse

Nothing moves.
Barefooted, my mind, walks over the facts.
Blind, bruise your fingers on the Braille of what is,
though, deaf, you do not know how to name it.

Yet patience. Sit down on the cold cushion of stillness.
Peer down your own depths where you hope to see
    something—
a face or at least a form that urges you forward—
unless with a sigh you get up, deciding
that walking alone is better than waiting out nothing.

Your soft soles and your fingers keep bleeding
as you gum your prayers, a mouth minus speech.

Nothing moves.

Minor Miner

One time
the poems lay loose like gold nuggets
spilling out of the pores of my skin.

Now I
hurtle down shafts of myself,
having become an abandoned mine,

where in
the dark, I, my lamp long gone out,
wait for the welding of rock with my bone.

Breakthrough

(On losing the best help I ever had)

Come back, my cool confusion,
my dear disorientation,
my lovely Lily of the Valley,
who doesn't know she's doomed,
or simply lacks illusion
with such a clean elation
no black alarm can rally
her homeless spirit homed.

Then let's all hold communion
instead of confrontation,
you Marys, Margarets, Megs,
you mothers, sisters, daughters;
it's family reunion
that finds by acclamation
we're sick of treading eggs.
More fun to walk deep waters!

About the Author

Vassar Miller lives in Houston, Texas. She was born there in 1924 and received her B.A. and M.A. degrees from the University of Houston. Her first book of poetry, *Adam's Footprint*, was published in 1956. Since then the Wesleyan University Press has published *Wage War on Silence, My Bones Being Wiser,* and *Onions and Roses.* Ms. Miller is currently at work on a novel and a collection of short stories. Besides writing, among her pleasures are "books and beer, friends and my two dogs—also my three-wheeled bike."